IF FOUND, PLEASE
RETURN THIS BOOK TO

....

OR CONTACT VIA EMAIL

....

UNION SQUARE & CO. and the distinctive Union Square & Co. logo are trademarks of Sterling Publishing Co., Inc.

Union Square & Co., LLC, is a subsidiary of Sterling Publishing Co., Inc.

ISBN 978-1-4549-5373-9

For information about custom editions, special sales, and premium purchases, please contact specialsales@unionsquareandco.com.

Printed in India

2 4 6 8 10 9 7 5 3 1

unionsquareandco.com

Design by Christine Heun and Nick Misani
Cover and interior illustrations by Nick Misani

THE ODYSSEY
TRAVEL
JOURNAL

The Odyssey Travel Journal

A
MEMORY BOOK
INSPIRED
BY THE
CLASSIC TALE OF ADVENTURE

ILLUSTRATION BY NICK MISANI

U
UNION
SQUARE
& CO.
NEW YORK

"Tell me, O Muse, of that ingenious hero who travelled far and wide after he had sacked the famous town of Troy. Many cities did he visit, and many were the nations with whose manners and customs he was acquainted."

HOW TO USE THIS JOURNAL

The *Odyssey*—the ancient tale of Ulysses, a wandering hero who, after ten years fighting in the Trojan War, spent another ten long years striving against angry gods, terrible beasts, and all manner of tempests and trials to reach his wife and son in Ithaca—is one of the world's first adventure stories. Originally written down in the seventh or eighth century BCE, and credited to the legendary blind poet Homer, it is purported to be much older than that—stemming from the ancient oral traditions of the region—mixing Greek myths with environments, cultures, and historical events (real and imagined).

It is also a travelogue—detailing one hero's encounter with foreign landscapes, cultures, and customs. There are evocative descriptions: the morning sun over the Mediterranean personified as "rosy-fingered Dawn," details of immense banquets like one at King Menelaus's stately golden hall, calves spit-roasted over flaming embers with the best cuts offered up to the gods. And terrible beasts like the one-eyed Cyclops or the "cruel and invincible" six-headed sea monster Scylla.

It's a rousing tale, a funny tale, a magical and wondrous tale—and the journal in your hands is designed to help you look at your own travels the way the bard Homer looked at the travels of Ulysses.

Throughout these pages, you'll find space to craft a one-of-a-kind memory book of your travels. It begins with a space to record the basic details of your trip: Where are you going? What are you packing? What is your itinerary and wish list?

The remainder of the journal's pages are open-ended, so there will be plenty of space for free journaling—recording overheard conversations, fleeting impressions, or day-to-day diary entries of where you are and where you are going. Throughout, like nuggets of hidden treasure, you'll find quotes from the *Odyssey* accompanied by guided prompts that will help you reflect in new and unexpected ways. Ulysses himself is a grand storyteller as well as a traveler—the quotes chosen here speak to the powerful storytelling qualities in the *Odyssey*—helping you transform your own memories into narrative.

Sometimes, you'll come across a quote on its own with no specific prompt—placed to help you connect to the spirit of adventure and discovery at the heart of the *Odyssey*. Throughout, don't feel the need to fill in every page all at once—a quote or prompt may not speak to you one day, but might spark a memory or an emotion on another.

The final pages of the journal offer a space to reflect on your return and what you gained, learned, and experienced.

While we don't expect you to be lost at sea for years on end or outwit a man-eating Cyclops like Ulysses did, we can take from the *Odyssey* a way of thinking about travel. Why not tell the story of our own lives as an adventure on the go? Why not infuse our days with meaning and humor and take record of all the kindnesses and challenges we encounter along the way? Let's invite our own muses to sing through us. . . .

A NOTE ON THE TRANSLATION

This journal uses the Victorian novelist Samuel Butler's definitive prose translation of the *Odyssey*, first published in 1900. Butler's version uses the Latin names for characters—for instance, our hero is named Ulysses rather than Odysseus, and the goddess of wisdom, Athena, is here called Minerva. Butler's vivid translation was one of two English translations James Joyce used as reference when he wrote his twentieth-century masterpiece, *Ulysses*.

PREPARATIONS

"There are many ships in Ithaca both old and new; I will run my eye over them for you and will choose the best; we will get her ready and will put out to sea without delay."

Use these pages to record initial thoughts about the journeys ahead of you. Feel free to be as brief or specific as you wish. Where are you going? How will you get there? Is it a road trip, a vacation? A backpacking adventure? What dates will you be gone? Are you going with friends or family or on your own?

List 5 experiences you hope to have on your trip.

1

2

3

4

5

What part of your planned trip excites you the most?
What part worries you the most?

PACKING LIST

Beyond the obvious essentials, list all the items here you wish to take with you on your trip. *(Don't forget your chargers and adapters!)*

ITINERARY

Record here the specifics of your trip, such as dates, locations, and events.

BEGINNINGS

"As the sail bellied out with the wind, the ship flew through the deep blue water, and the foam hissed against her bows as she sped onward."

DATE: / / LOCATION:

The beginning of an adventure and the end of an adventure contain much for contemplation and recordkeeping. At the start, all is possibility and anticipation. Write here your impressions of your first day of travel.

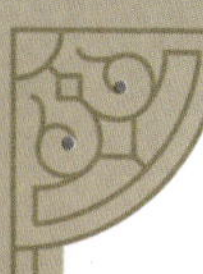

"She bound on her glittering golden sandals, imperishable, with which she can fly like the wind over land or sea; she grasped the redoubtable bronze-shod spear, so stout and sturdy and strong, wherewith she quells the ranks of heroes who have displeased her, and down she darted from the topmost summits of Olympus."

Minerva, the Goddess of Wisdom, and the patron to the hero Ulysses, left the paradise of Olympus to compel Ulysses's son, Telemachus, to himself leave the comforts of his home to find news of his long-lost father. What place are you leaving as you begin your trip? What comforts and which people will you miss while you are gone?

DATE: / / LOCATION:

DATE: / / LOCATION:

DATE: / / LOCATION:

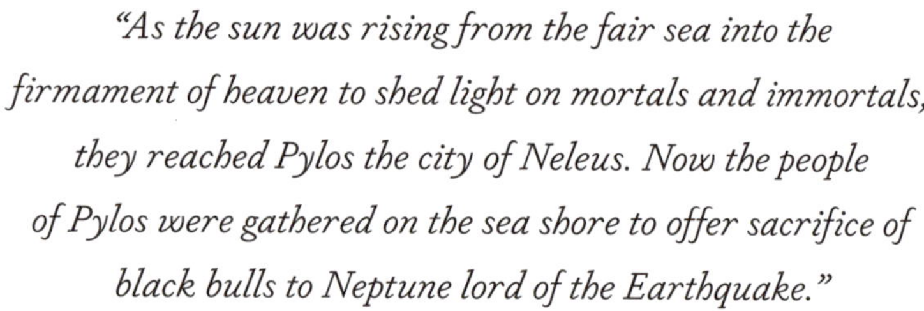

"As the sun was rising from the fair sea into the firmament of heaven to shed light on mortals and immortals, they reached Pylos the city of Neleus. Now the people of Pylos were gathered on the sea shore to offer sacrifice of black bulls to Neptune lord of the Earthquake."

Tasked by Minerva to find news of his father, Telemachus sails to the island of Pylos, home to Nestor, an old friend of his father's. The first sight he sees is a great feast upon the island's shores. On your own journey, what is the first sight you see? Is it from a plane window, or the dark parking lot of a hotel at midnight? Write a few sentences here about your first impressions of your destination.

DATE: / / LOCATION:

DATE: / / LOCATION:

Use this space to doodle, scribble, make a list, or draw a map.

DATE: / / LOCATION:

DATE: / / LOCATION:

DATE: / / LOCATION:

OBSERVATIONS
NEAR & FAR
"And Ulysses answered, 'King Alcinous, it is a good thing to hear a bard with such a divine voice as this man has. There is nothing better or more delightful than when a whole people make merry together . . . while the table is loaded with bread and meats, and the cup-bearer draws wine and fills his cup for every man.'"

DATE: / / LOCATION:

Now that your journey has begun, use these following pages to record as you see fit—jot down notes or observations, questions and wishes. Use the quotes and prompts as inspiration, but don't feel compelled to answer each in turn.

DATE: / / LOCATION:

DATE: / / LOCATION:

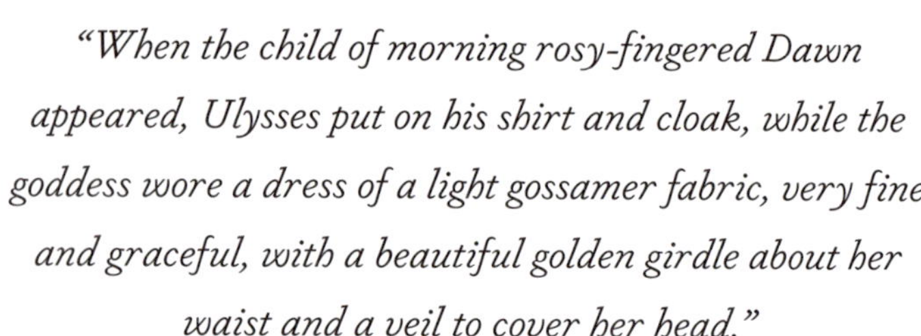

"When the child of morning rosy-fingered Dawn appeared, Ulysses put on his shirt and cloak, while the goddess wore a dress of a light gossamer fabric, very fine and graceful, with a beautiful golden girdle about her waist and a veil to cover her head."

Take a moment to think about clothing. What sort of clothing are you wearing on your trip? Hiking gear or beachwear? Did you pack formal attire for an event?

Or did you buy special clothes for the trip? Describe them here. And what about those around you? Spend some time people-watching to see if you can find common items of clothing or accessories that passersby have on. Note one example below.

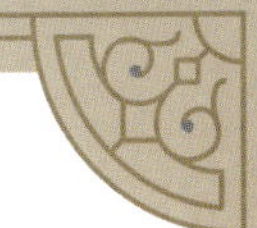

DATE: / / LOCATION:

DATE: / / LOCATION:

DATE: / / LOCATION:

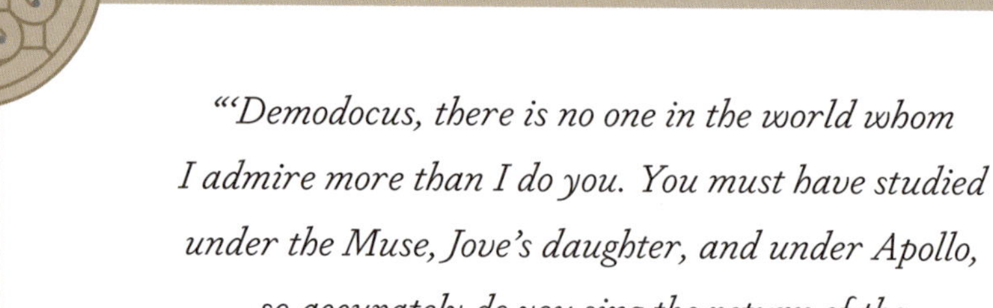

"'Demodocus, there is no one in the world whom I admire more than I do you. You must have studied under the Muse, Jove's daughter, and under Apollo, so accurately do you sing the return of the Achaeans with all their sufferings and adventures.'"

In the palace of the Phaeacians, Ulysses (who has not yet told the court his name) is moved to tears by the song of the blind poet Demodocus, who weaves tales of the Trojan War and of the trials Ulysses and his comrades had faced in the conflict. What arts and entertainments have you encountered thus far that have moved you? Make note of anything from a street busker to a visit to a museum to a campfire ghost story.

DATE: / / LOCATION:

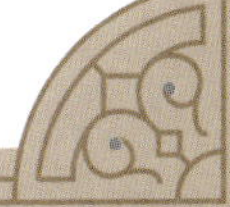

DATE: / / LOCATION:

DATE: / / LOCATION:

Use this space to doodle, scribble, make a list, or draw a map.

"We brought our ship into a safe harbour without a word, for some god guided us thither, and having landed we lay there for two days and two nights, worn out in body and mind."

DATE: / / LOCATION:

DATE: / / LOCATION:

DATE: / / LOCATION:

DATE: / / LOCATION:

DATE: / / LOCATION:

"We waited the whole morning and made the best of it, watching the seals come up in hundreds to bask upon the sea shore, till at noon the old man of the sea came up too, and when he had found his fat seals he went over them and counted them."

Trapped on an island off the coast of Egypt, Ulysses observed Proteus, a water spirit, come ashore to tend to his herd of seals. Whether you're in the city or the suburbs, on a camping trip or a cruise, nature is buzzing and moving and scurrying about you. Observe the natural world, and if you have moments of leisure, try, like Ulysses, to observe long enough to see rhythms emerge—perhaps it's a bird flying back and forth from its nest, or the movement of clouds across the sky.

DATE: / / LOCATION:

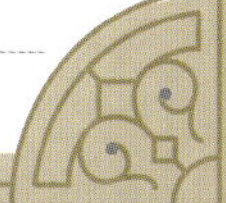

DATE: / / LOCATION:

DATE: / / LOCATION:

"'And now, O queen, have pity upon me, for you are the first person I have met, and I know no one else in this country. Show me the way to your town. May heaven grant you in all things your heart's desire.'"

DATE: / / LOCATION:

DATE: / / LOCATION:

DATE: / / LOCATION:

Use this space to doodle, scribble, make a list, or draw a map.

"Mercury, guide and guardian, bound on his glittering golden sandals with which he could fly like the wind over land and sea. Then he swooped down through the firmament till he reached the level of the sea, whose waves he skimmed like a cormorant that flies fishing every hole and corner of the ocean, and drenching its thick plumage in the spray."

DATE: / / LOCATION:

DATE: / / LOCATION:

DATE: / / LOCATION:

"A vine loaded with grapes was trained and grew luxuriantly about the mouth of the cave; there were also four running rills of water in channels cut pretty close together, and turned hither and thither so as to irrigate the beds of violets and luscious herbage over which they flowed. Even a god could not help being charmed with such a lovely spot."

DATE: / / LOCATION:

DATE: / / LOCATION:

DATE: / / LOCATION:

CONNECTIONS

"'Ulysses, noble son of Laertes, tell your men to leave off crying; I know how much you have all of you suffered at sea, and how ill you have fared, but that is over now, so stay here, and eat and drink till you are once more as strong and hearty as you were when you left Ithaca.'"

DATE: / / LOCATION:

Whether you are traveling solo, or with friends or family—or for work, school, or pleasure—any journey from home is made more enriching by the connections you make with your companions or those you meet along the way. The prompts in this section will help you note the moments of friendship and kindness that make a trip something special.

DATE: / / LOCATION:

DATE: / / LOCATION:

"'And now for yourself—stay here some ten or twelve days longer, and I will then speed you on your way. I will make you a noble present of a chariot and three horses. I will also give you a beautiful chalice that so long as you live you may think of me whenever you make a drink-offering to the immortal gods.'"

Throughout the *Odyssey*, we witness the courtesy of hosts to their guests on numerous occasions (as well as a few memorable instances of discourtesy). Where on your trip have you experienced hospitality in an unexpected place? Where do you wish you'd been shown more courtesy?

DATE: / / LOCATION:

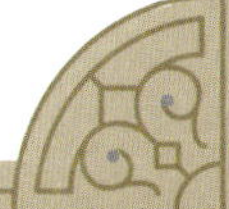

DATE: / / LOCATION:

Use this space to doodle, scribble, make a list, or draw a map.

DATE: / / LOCATION:

DATE: / / LOCATION:

DATE: / / LOCATION:

"'Stranger,' said she, 'rise and let us be going back to the town; I will introduce you at the house of my excellent father, where I can tell you that you will meet all the best people among the Phaeacians.'"

DATE: / / LOCATION:

DATE: / / LOCATION:

DATE: / / LOCATION:

"As soon as she had done washing me and anointing me with oil, she arrayed me in a good cloak and shirt and led me to a richly decorated seat inlaid with silver. A maid servant then brought me water in a beautiful golden ewer and poured it into a silver basin for me to wash my hands, and she drew a clean table beside me; an upper servant brought me bread and offered me many things of what there was in the house."

Luxury and indulgences come in many forms and are often hallmarks of a vacation or pleasure trip. What form of luxury have you experienced thus far in your travels? What about simple luxuries, like an unhurried cup of coffee, or a pleasant talk with a friend?

DATE: / / LOCATION:

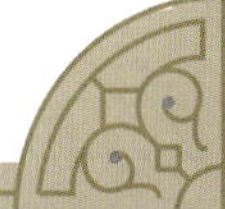

DATE: / / LOCATION:

DATE: / / LOCATION:

DATE: / / LOCATION:

DATE: / / LOCATION:

"The king was delighted at this, and exclaimed, 'Aldermen and town councillors, our guest seems to be a person of singular judgement; let us give him such proof of our hospitality as he may reasonably expect. There are twelve chief men among you, and counting myself there are thirteen; contribute, each of you, a clean cloak, a shirt, and a talent of fine gold; let us give him all this in a lump down at once, so that when he gets his supper he may do so with a light heart.'"

DATE: / / LOCATION:

DATE: / / LOCATION:

DATE: / / LOCATION:

Use this space to doodle, scribble, make a list, or draw a map.

"'Hear me, O King, whoever you may be, and save me from the anger of the sea-god Neptune, for I approach you prayerfully. Any one who has lost his way has at all times a claim even upon the gods, wherefore in my distress I draw near to your stream, and cling to the knees of your riverhood. Have mercy upon me, O king, for I declare myself your suppliant.'"

Here, Ulysses, lost at sea and endlessly dashed against a rocky shore by the tempestuous waves, appealed to the spirit of the river inlet he was swimming toward. The spirit answers him and calms the waters, giving him safe passage to the island. What help have you asked for on your journey? Was it answered? By strangers or by friends?

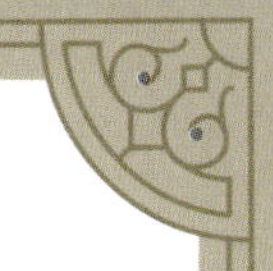

DATE: / / LOCATION:

DATE: / / LOCATION:

DATE: / / LOCATION:

"When we reached the harbour we found it land-locked under steep cliffs, with a narrow entrance between two headlands. My captains took all their ships inside, and made them fast close to one another, for there was never so much as a breath of wind inside, but it was always dead calm."

DATE: / / LOCATION:

DATE: / / LOCATION:

DATE: / / LOCATION:

"'Sir,' answered Telemachus, 'it has been very kind of you to talk to me in this way, as though I were your own son, and I will do all you tell me; I know you want to be getting on with your voyage, but stay a little longer till you have taken a bath and refreshed yourself. I will then give you a present, and you shall go on your way rejoicing; I will give you one of great beauty and value—a keepsake such as only dear friends give to one another.'"

A major lesson of the *Odyssey* is that more important than the hospitality you receive is the kindness and generosity you show to strangers, as here Telemachus does to the goddess Minerva, who is disguised as an unassuming old man. Make note of how you have been actively generous on this trip, and list five ways you can be more so for the remainder of your voyage.

DATE: / / LOCATION:

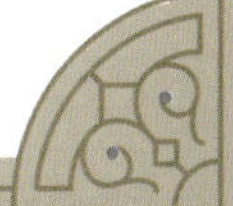

"'Young men,' said he, 'come up to that throw if you can, and I will throw another disc as heavy or even heavier. If anyone wants to have a bout with me let him come on . . . I will box, wrestle, or run, I do not care what it is, with any man of you all except Laodamas, but not with him because I am his guest, and one cannot compete with one's own personal friend.'"

DATE: / / LOCATION:

TRIALS & TRAVAILS
"'We Cyclops do not care about Jove or any
of your blessed gods, for we are ever so much stronger
than they. I shall not spare either yourself
or your companions out of any regard for Jove,
unless I am in the humour for doing so.'"

DATE: / / LOCATION:

On his journey across the Mediterranean, Ulysses was beset by a succession of hardships, shipwrecks, monsters, and sorcerers. We can hope no such trials await you, but no voyage is without its challenges—and challenges, after all, make for a good story. In this section, you'll be asked to detail the challenges you have faced and how you overcame them.

"But we suffered much more than this; what mortal tongue indeed could tell the whole story? Though you were to stay here and question me for five years, or even six, I could not tell you all that the Achaeans suffered, and you would turn homeward weary of my tale before it ended."

DATE: / / LOCATION:

DATE: / / LOCATION:

Use this space to doodle, scribble, make a list, or draw a map.

DATE: / / LOCATION:

"They sang these words most musically, and as I longed to hear them further I made signs by frowning to my men that they should set me free; but they quickened their stroke, and Eurylochus and Perimedes bound me with still stronger bonds till we had got out of hearing of the Sirens' voices."

DATE: / / LOCATION:

DATE: / / LOCATION:

DATE: / / LOCATION:

"'Ulysses is indeed dead, still do not press me to marry again immediately, wait . . . till I have completed a pall for the hero Laertes, to be in readiness against the time when death shall take him.' We assented; whereon we could see her working on her great web all day long, but at night she would unpick the stitches again by torchlight. She fooled us in this way for three years and we never found her out."

Not to be outshone by the craftiness of her husband, Penelope herself showed cunning and strategy in keeping away the unscrupulous suitors who wished her to remarry. By day she wove a death shroud for her father-in-law, promising she would remarry upon its completion, and at night she would pull apart her work. List a few times on your trip that you have used strategy and skill in unique ways.

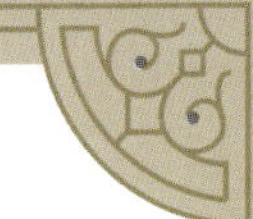

DATE: / / LOCATION:

DATE: / / LOCATION:

DATE: /   /   LOCATION:

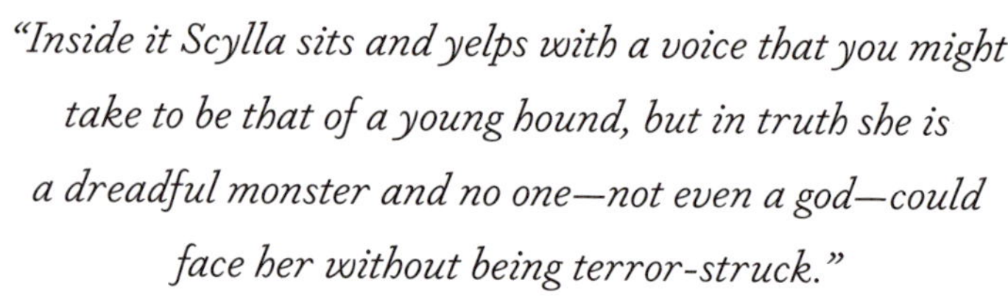

"Inside it Scylla sits and yelps with a voice that you might take to be that of a young hound, but in truth she is a dreadful monster and no one—not even a god—could face her without being terror-struck."

The six-headed sea-beast Scylla was one of the most horrific obstacles Ulysses had to overcome—which he did by careful planning and following the advice of the gods. What setbacks have you avoided with planning or just by good luck?

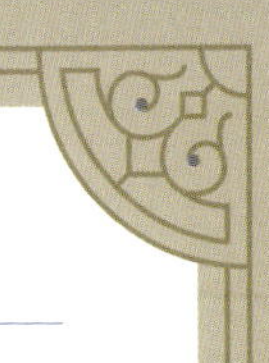

DATE: / / LOCATION:

DATE: / / LOCATION:

DATE: / / LOCATION:

"Then we entered the Straits in great fear of mind, for on the one hand was Scylla, and on the other dread Charybdis kept sucking up the salt water. As she vomited it up, it was like the water in a cauldron when it is boiling over upon a great fire."

DATE: / / LOCATION:

DATE: / / LOCATION:

DATE: / / LOCATION:

"As he spoke Jove sent two eagles from the top of the mountain, and they flew on and on with the wind, sailing side by side in their own lordly flight. When they were right over the middle of the assembly they wheeled and circled about, beating the air with their wings and glaring death into the eyes of them that were below."

DATE: / / LOCATION:

DATE: / / LOCATION:

DATE: / / LOCATION:

Use this space to doodle, scribble, make a list, or draw a map.

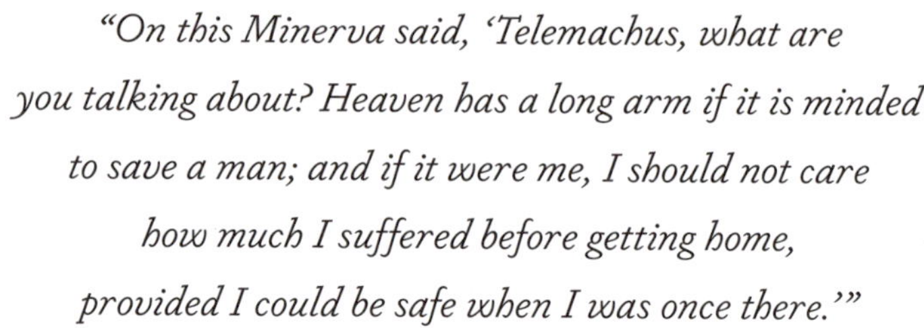

"On this Minerva said, 'Telemachus, what are you talking about? Heaven has a long arm if it is minded to save a man; and if it were me, I should not care how much I suffered before getting home, provided I could be safe when I was once there.'"

Throughout the *Odyssey*, Minerva provides guidance to both Ulysses and his son Telemachus (who is on his own adventure). In Telemachus, she instills self-confidence in his own abilities and a trust in the ways of the gods. What have been some of the primary lessons or unexpected ideas you have encountered?

DATE: / / LOCATION:

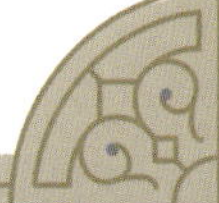

DATE: / / LOCATION:

DATE: / / LOCATION:

"Then they went away, and I laughed inwardly at the success of my clever stratagem, but the Cyclops, groaning and in an agony of pain, felt about with his hands till he found the stone and took it from the door; then he sat in the doorway and stretched his hands in front of it to catch anyone going out with the sheep, for he thought I might be foolish enough to attempt this."

DATE: / / LOCATION:

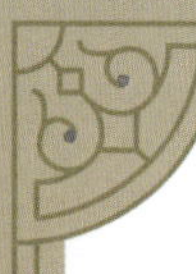

"When she had got them into her house, she set them upon benches and seats and mixed them a mess with cheese, honey, meal, and Pramnian wine, but she drugged it with wicked poisons to make them forget their homes, and when they had drunk she turned them into pigs by a stroke of her wand, and shut them up in her pig-styes."

On Circe's enchanted isle, the sorceress tricked Ulysses's crew and turned them into pigs. Ulysses used his eloquence and wits to beseech Circe to transform them back into humans. Wits and guile are essential tools when on the go. Where have you talked yourself into (or out of) a pleasant or unpleasant situation?

DATE: / / LOCATION:

HOMEWARD BOUND

"'Nevertheless, I want to get home, and can think of nothing else. If some god wrecks me when I am on the sea, I will bear it and make the best of it. I have had infinite trouble both by land and sea already, so let this go with the rest.'"

DATE: / / LOCATION:

The *Odyssey's* central narrative is one of homecoming, and while your voyage may have a different end goal, as you near your return, it's time to take stock of your time away, and also savor every last minute of your adventure.

The prompts here will help you reflect on all you have experienced on whatever road you may be traveling upon.

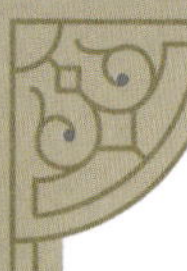

"Moreover, she made the wind fair and warm for him, and gladly did Ulysses spread his sail before it, while he sat and guided the raft skilfully by means of the rudder. He never closed his eyes, but kept them fixed on the Pleiads, on late-setting Bootes, and on the Bear—which men also call the wain, and which turns round and round where it is, facing Orion."

When Ulysses was finally released from the nymph Calypso's island, he sailed toward home on a makeshift raft. What conveyance will get you home? List here all the vehicles you've taken thus far on this trip. Canoes? Scooters? Taxicabs? Bicycles? Try to describe each travel experience in detail.

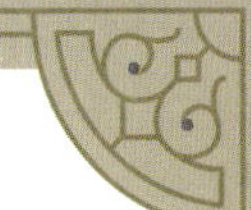

DATE: / / LOCATION:

DATE: / / LOCATION:

DATE: / / LOCATION:

"And Ulysses said, 'Nausicaa, daughter of great Alcinous, may Jove the mighty husband of Juno, grant that I may reach my home; so shall I bless you as my guardian angel all my days, for it was you who saved me.'"

DATE: / / LOCATION:

DATE: / / LOCATION:

Use this space to doodle, scribble, make a list, or draw a map.

DATE: / / LOCATION:

"'As for you, Achilles, no one was ever yet so fortunate as you have been, nor ever will be, for you were adored by all us Argives as long as you were alive, and now that you are here you are a great prince among the dead.'"

Ulysses was compelled to visit Hades, the land of the dead, to seek prophecy of his return voyage. There he met many comrades and heroes who beseeched him to remember and honor them upon his return to Ithaca. What memories and friendships will you wish to honor and remember when your voyage is complete?

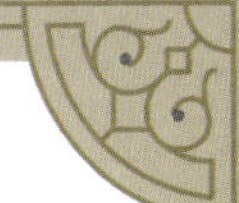

DATE: / / LOCATION:

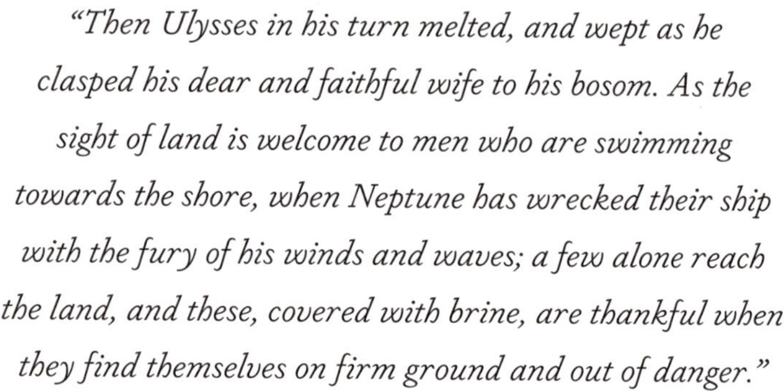

"Then Ulysses in his turn melted, and wept as he clasped his dear and faithful wife to his bosom. As the sight of land is welcome to men who are swimming towards the shore, when Neptune has wrecked their ship with the fury of his winds and waves; a few alone reach the land, and these, covered with brine, are thankful when they find themselves on firm ground and out of danger."

For some, it's the sight of a familiar skyline, for others the friendly face awaiting you at home—list a few things you are looking forward to at the end of your trip.

DATE: / / LOCATION:

“When they saw Ulysses and were certain it was he, they stood there lost in astonishment; but Ulysses scolded them good naturedly and said, ‘Sit down to your dinner, old man, and never mind about your surprise; we have been wanting to begin for some time and have been waiting for you.’”

DATE: / / LOCATION:

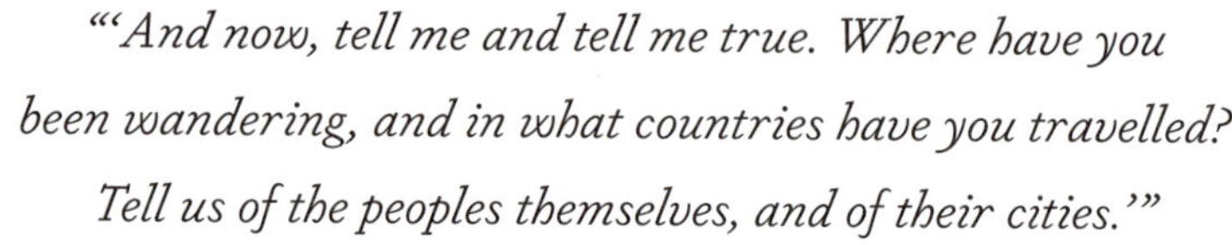

"'And now, tell me and tell me true. Where have you been wandering, and in what countries have you travelled? Tell us of the peoples themselves, and of their cities.'"

Where to next? Along with final thoughts on the end of your own odyssey, write out a dream list of places to visit and things to experience.

DATE: / / LOCATION:

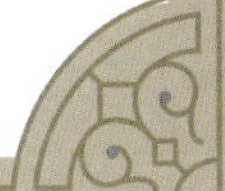

DATE: / / LOCATION: